14th Sept 2010

Xenophobe's®
guide to the
ESTONIANS

Hilary Bird
Lembit Öpik
Ulvi Mustmaa

To Clive & Caroline,

A pl... ... ...

on t...

addr...

heep ... ...!

GW00645278

...

O
Oval Books

Published by Oval Books
5 St John's Buildings
Canterbury Crescent
London SW9 7QH

Telephone: +44 (0)20 7733 8585
E-mail: info@ovalbooks.com
Web site: www.ovalbooks.com

Published 2010

Editor – Catriona Tulloch Scott
Series Editor – Anne Tauté

Cover designer – Vicki Towers
Printer – J.F. Print Ltd., Sparkford, Somerset
Producer – Oval Projects Ltd.

Cover: a Lenovo Ideapad S10 laptop
with traditional Estonian folk pattern
by kind permission of Elisa Eesti AS.

Xenophobe's® is a Registered Trademark.

For his advice and ideas, grateful thanks
are given to Tiit Heidmets.

ISBN: 978-1-906042-30-1

Contents

The population of Estonia is 1.3 million, compared with 2.2 million Latvians, 3.5 million Lithuanians, 82 million Germans, 140 million Russians and 307 million Americans.

Estonia is slightly bigger than Denmark and has a coastline fragmented with 1,521 islands. Legend has it that a giant who lived on the second largest island wanted to link it to the largest one to visit his family and friends, so he threw stones into the sea to create a causeway. It was never finished.

Nationalism & Identity

Forewarned

Although Estonia is a young nation, the Estonians are not a young people. Heaped on the bedrock of prehistoric origins are layers and layers of cultures and traditions either adapted or lifted lock, stock and barrel from the many invaders who have ruled the Estonian roost for the better part of the last millennium. This melange congealed at some time during the Soviet era into a romanticised ideal of what Estonians were like when Estonians were really Estonian – hardworking, honest and severe, living a simple life on the land and squabbling with their neighbours as depicted in the great Estonian novel *Truth and Justice*, an everyday story of hardship, gritty perseverance, and swamp drainage.

> **❝ Although Estonia is a young nation, the Estonians are not a young people. ❞**

Although the Estonian tribes have lived on their own lands for 10,000 years, 700 of these nameless years were spent in slavery. There was no history of Estonia before 1918 because there was no Estonian nation.

National Pride

Estonian national pride is demonstrated in national symbols – the national flag (each house has a bracket for the blue, black and white tricolour that is trotted

1

out on high days and holidays), the national coat of arms (three lions *passant*), the national bird (the barn swallow), the national stone (limestone), the national drink (beer), the national food (pork, potatoes and cabbage), and so on.

> **66 Estonians see themselves as tough, stern, self-sufficient northern people – the last of the Vikings. 99**

All these things, according to the Estonians, are 'pure' Estonian. Never mind that France, Italy, Russia and Germany have tricolours, never mind that the coat of arms strongly resembles that of Denmark, never mind that the national bird nests all over Europe, that the national flower – the cornflower – is scattered in cornfields throughout Europe, that their national drink is quaffed all over the world, or that the common spud was embraced everywhere in the mid 19th century. The important thing is that these items are now firmly entrenched in the modern Estonian psyche as exclusively and uniquely Estonian. Do not try and argue. It's an utter waste of time; you simply will not be believed.

How they see themselves

Estonians see themselves as tough, stern, self-sufficient northern people – the last of the Vikings. It is even posited that the word 'Viking' comes from the Estonian '*vee king*' meaning 'water shoe' and referring to the shoe-shaped hulls of their wooden boats. The Swedes, the Norwegians and the Danes may play down their violent past but the Estonians remember with pride the capture of a Swedish queen by warrior Estonian tribes on a raid in 1187.

Real Estonians are tough. The men eat meat, drink strong beer and down glasses of vodka in one gulp. They use a dry lavatory at the end

> **66 In their heart of hearts the Estonians know they are odd and don't quite fit the standard Euro-model – or any other. 99**

of a frozen, slippery path in the dead of winter and don't even think about soft toilet paper.

Estonians look affectionately on their fictitious national hero – a naive, laddish figure called the 'Son of Kalev'. He appears regularly in the media clad in his linen tunic and little brimless Estonian cap, his beer paunch hanging over a belt covered in ancient symbols, grinning cheerfully and waving his blood sausage (national food) as he strides towards the Eiffel Tower, the Colosseum, Big Ben and the Brandenburg Gate to take Estonia's place amongst the family of European nations. But, in their heart of hearts the Estonians know they are odd and don't quite fit the standard Euro-model – or any other, for that matter.

Estonian individuality was demonstrated admirably at an International Architecture Biennial in Venice. Amongst the outpourings of serious contemporary offerings, the Estonian pavilion proudly fielded a display of dry toilets – outhouses – that ranged from a glass cubicle (thankfully opaque) lit by candles standing in a field of snow, to a rustic Pegasus which one entered beneath a raised twig tail.

'Tis a small thing but mine own

Small is beautiful to an Estonian and 'Everything is local' is a slogan guaranteed to sell anything. Estonians would read the telephone directory with the rapt attention commanded by a great thriller if it was the directory of their own home town.

The Estonians are determined that whatever has been salvaged from their turbulent past that is 100% Estonian (and there's not a lot) will be preserved. Hence their insistence that would-be citizens speak a modicum of Estonian. It is when Estonians speak and, more especially, sing, that they connect with their ancient birthright.

> **66 Estonians would read the telephone directory... if it was the directory of their own home town. 99**

Folk culture constantly reminds them that 'my little home is tiny but is big enough for the missus, the kids, the pig, dog, cat and me'. The British may sing about ruling the waves, the Americans about amber waves of grain, but Estonian national songs laud the local pond, the cherry tree in the yard and their very own boulder in the Baltic Sea.

How they see others

For centuries the Estonians loathed the Germans, the first people to intrude on their freedom and disenfranchise them in their own lands. The sins of the Germans, however, paled into insignificance in the 20th century when Estonia was annexed into the USSR. The Soviet Russians did what had been impossible for 700 years. They made the Estonians love the Germans.

Much as they would like to, Estonians cannot ignore their Eastern neighbour. There are 140 million Russian citizens living next door making a scary ratio of 1:140 in favour of The Bear. Estonians feel that, at best, Russians are a noisy, sloppy lot, always on the bottle, producing bad quality goods and with gardens full of weeds. All Estonians agree that Russians are unpredictable and not to be trusted.

> **66 There are 140 million Russian citizens living next door making a scary ratio of 1:140 in favour of The Bear. 99**

The presence in Estonia of ethnic Russians (just under three out of every ten residents) whose loyalty is far from assured makes the Estonians even twitchier. Tension between the two communities rarely develops into bloody-nose territory. Serious clashes usually come at a much higher level, when Moscow decides to admonish its erstwhile colony as if it was an errant child. The exception that proved the rule was a riot of (mostly) young Russians that attended the removal in

2007 of 'the metal man' (a Soviet-era war memorial) from the centre of Tallinn, followed by a wave of violent protests outside Estonian embassies in Russia. But this was only one side of the story. The morning after the outburst, anxious and vastly outnumbered ethnic Estonians in a tower block in Tallinn woke up to find that their Russian neighbours had left little bunches of flowers outside their front doors by way of apology.

❝ The Estonians see the Finns as rather stuffy and call them *põder* (moose). ❞

Relations with Finland are cordial. Finnish TV served as a window to the free world for 50 years and practically every Estonian has been to Finland. The Estonians see the Finns as rather stuffy and call them *põder* (moose) because they are large, loud and have clumsy mating habits. Helsinki is only 53 km from Tallinn and there is considerable cultural and commercial exchange. There is also an exchange of quite another sort. For many years, Finns have evaded sky-high taxes on alcohol in their own country by making a weekend 'booze cruise' to Tallinn where liquor costs considerably less.

The British arrived in droves, too, once cheap airfares became available, and for a while Tallinn experienced a phenomenon of waking up to find stag party members comatose on their national monuments. Estonians tolerate all these drinking invasions because they are very profitable – the revellers seemingly determined to drink industrial quantities of alcohol.

Estonians have a good relationship with Latvia and Lithuania, the two other Baltic States. A sense of camaraderie still lingers from the time of the 'Singing Revolution' of the late 1980s, when the three Baltic midgets, all annexed unwillingly in 1944, took on the might of the USSR. The most impressive manifestation of their discontent was the Baltic Chain of 1989, a two-million person protest involving the linking of hands from Tallinn, through Latvia and ending in Vilnius, Lithuania. The Baltic States have traded cheese and sausage and voted for one another in the Eurovision Song Contest ever since.

How they would like to be seen

Most Estonians can hardly contain their indifference to life beyond their borders and would like not to be seen at all. The attention of others has usually led to Big Trouble.

Older Estonians would like to be seen, when visible, as cultured and book literate. Young Estonians would like to be seen as clever computer-literate

66 Most Estonians would like not to be seen at all. The attention of others has usually led to Big Trouble. 99

technocrats. This is because Estonia has embraced new technology with a will. The reason is simple: it is cold for three months of the year and freezing for another three (and, as the saying goes, 'bad skiing weather' for the rest), so no-one in their right mind would make a journey in sub-zero temperatures when they could use a phone or send an e-mail.

Beyond the glass and steel towers of Tallinn the country may look quaint and serene, but 21st-century microchips lurk everywhere: the Estonians, from tots to pensioners, are wired. While Moscow was in charge an East German washing machine, when available, took up half the house and required strengthening of the foundations. Soviet stagnation meant that the Estonians missed out on an entire generation of smart inventions. But once they secured their freedom they stocked up on all the latest and smartest of everything.

> **66 21st-century microchips lurk everywhere: the Estonians, from tots to pensioners, are wired. 99**

In modern e-Stonia it is possible to e-park your car, do e-business and e-banking, amongst other e-activities. 80% of Estonians have mobile phones, more than 70% file their taxes on the Internet and even petrol stations in Tallinn are equipped with WiFi (e-wireless) connections. It's not just the urban suited and booted who make full use of the country's mobile phone networks, Internet and WiFi connections: rural communities, small towns and remote island farmhouses are all wired up. The talk among elderly ladies at the village shop is not about the weather or crops, but about the upset caused by a 20-minute disconnection to the Internet provider in some households the day before. Farmer Andrus will sit on his 60-year-old tractor ordering a spare part from a company miles away, fisherman Peet's wife will ring him from the supermarket while he is bobbing around in the Baltic to ask what he wants to eat tonight. Even animals get in on the act. Electronically tagged dairy cows are fitted with equipment so sophisticated that if the animal is off colour the computer won't let it be milked.

How others see them

The Russians see Estonia as one of All the Russias because they ruled it for over 200 years and old habits die hard.

The Scandinavians have an 'elder brother' attitude to Estonia. This is because they own most of it: 95% of the Estonian banking system

> **❝ The Russians see Estonia as one of All the Russias because they ruled it for over 200 years and old habits die hard. ❞**

belongs to Scandinavian groups. The Swedes make up some 55% of foreign investors and the Finns around 25%. The same applies in the opposite direction. Estonia's main trading partner for exports is Finland at 19%, with Sweden weighing in at 12% and Russia at 11%. Other partners include the other Baltic States, other Scandinavians and the Dutch.

For those countries not in Scandinavia or the Russian Federation, Estonia is perceived as part of Russia or totally off the radar. Estonian soldiers who served in Iraq had a common complaint: no-one knew where they were from. Many of their American colleagues had never even heard of Estonia or thought it was a mythical country. The Iraqis hadn't a clue either. One Estonian captain gave up – "I told them I was from the moon," he said.

Character

Estonian characteristics were first enshrined in *Kalevipoeg* (*The Son of Kalev*), the national epic. The Son of Kalev (SOK) is an intellectually challenged giant. His father is Kalev, 'a mighty man'. The Son of Kalev wins the throne of Estonia in a stone-throwing competition (forget chess or even cutting a complicated knot in half, a battle of wits is quite out of the question). SOK may not be strong on brains but he has plenty of brawn. Having raised a few townships and ploughed the Estonian lands single-handed, he builds a boat and sets off on a voyage of discovery. At the end of the world he finds, not a romantic, enchanted kingdom, but a brick wall.

66 At the end of the world he finds, not a romantic, enchanted kingdom, but a brick wall. 99

After poking his finger through a hole he laughs and returns south saying that he's learnt a lot from the experience. Quite what is difficult to discern since he loses the battle with the 'iron men from the south' despite his great strength, is outwitted, gets his legs chopped off when, in a careless moment, he forgets the terms of a critical curse, bleeds to death, ascends to Valhalla, then is dragged away from a booze-up with the lads and sent to guard hell. The legend tells that Estonia will thrive when the Son of Kalev returns. No-one tries to explain why.

> **To be called 'stubborn' is a great compliment for Estonians.**

There is a little of the SOK in every Estonian man. A Son of Kalev is not romantic. He is devoted to his mum, he is hard working, loyal, brave, a good sport, a man who keeps his word and, most of all, stubborn. To be called 'stubborn' is a great compliment for Estonians. There is deep admiration for the determination to carry on whether or not the odds are insuperable and it is stupid even to *think* about doing so.

It's normal to be 'normal'

Nothing is ever 'wonderful' or 'great' to an Estonian. Things are always a laconic 'usual' or, more normally, 'normal'. When an Estonian says that something is 'normal' it indicates that life is continuing on a safe, well-trodden path and that this is the way things should be. Too much excitement is treated as suspect. Essentially the Estonians agree with the Chinese curse: 'May you live in exciting times.'

Let's wait and see

The roots of *'Ootame, vaatame'* 'Let's wait and see', are embedded in the deepest chasm of the Estonian psyche because, for a very long time, the people had little choice to do anything else. An 18th-century serf could wake up one morning, be swapped for a hunting hound, and end up somewhere far far away by nightfall, never to see his family again. Making plans was pointless and, as the malpractices of the 18th-century Germans were resumed by the 20th-century Soviets, the habit of not committing oneself to definite arrangements has stuck.

> **The roots of *'Ootame, vaatame'*, 'Let's wait and see', are embedded in the deepest chasm of the Estonian psyche.**

This philosophy is a close relation to the Spanish *mañana* ('tomorrow'). The difference is that the languid Spanish are just deferring something. The pragmatic Estonians are not. They are waiting and seeing. Harsh experience has taught them that it's useless to waste energy fretting over Fate.

The Estonians waited and saw out seven centuries of occupations with only three major mass uprisings –

the St. George's Night Rebellion of 1343-45, the War of Independence of 1918-20, and the Singing Revolution of 1988. But when the waiting and seeing is over (usually a few eons), then a lot of patience is a lot of patience to lose, and the Estonians will embrace their fate with a reckless courage and conviction. Once their dander is up, they are out of the trap like a greyhound.

Melancholy musings

Inside every Estonian there is a melancholy sigh. It is a long, quiet exhalation of breath redolent with sorrow, as if some tragedy or loss is recalled from the gallery of Estonian collective consciousness. Aaahhh... It is particularly noticeable with the aged but, as the young grow up, they find themselves trading their exuberance for that same mantle of solemnity.

66 When life is going swimmingly, Estonians merely assume trouble must surely be on its way. 99

When Estonians look to the horizon, they are looking not only into the distance but into the past. There has been too much sorrow in the land to risk forgetting one's ancestors or one's history. It is vital to maintain a quiet vigil, lest to drop their guard allows the trouble to return.

When life is going swimmingly, Estonians merely assume trouble must surely be on its way. Thus, when the going is easy, they are drawn to reflect upon past travails. "Well, yes, this may be a beautiful and calm summer's day," eulogises Kalle the fisherman, "but I remember clearly how, 20 years ago, my grandfather was on this very same lake. An unexpected storm arose and the boat sank… he was nearly drowned in the icy waters (wistful shaking of head whilst staring at some unidentified point in the far distance). Aaahhh…"

Lateral thinking

Lateral thinking (the ability to conceive ideas without using step-by-step logic) is a very Estonian trait. Alphabetical or numerical order does not occur as a matter of course. Number two does not necessarily come after number one in the Estonian mindset. Books do not automatically have an index or, if they do, they have one with a rationale that is difficult to fathom. This all stems from the structure of the language. A paragraph of Estonian text is best tackled as a jigsaw puzzle. All the elements of a formula are present but not in any order comprehensible to non-Estonians.

66 Number two does not necessarily come after number one in the Estonian mindset. 99

Estonian time management is a mystery. Estonians never do more than one thing at a time, and the one

14

thing is done with absolute concentration and with meticulous attention to detail and as if they had all the time in the world. This appearance of snail-like activity is deceptive. If they really want to do something, such as organize a song festival with gigantic choirs, or mobilize an army of volunteers to clean up illegally-dumped litter in forests, meadows and rivers all over the country, it gets done. Do not ask the Estonians to explain. They don't know either.

Manners & Behaviour

Silence and solitude

Silence is golden to an Estonian. Deep down in their souls they crave for the vast, silent spaces of the ancestors who, carried there on the wings of birds, dwell for all eternity in the Milky Way pinning stars to the firmament.

Estonians are taciturn. 'Let your face be like ice' goes an old folk adage. Don't expect a chatty taxi driver on your drive

> **66 Estonians are taciturn. 'Let your face be like ice' goes an old folk adage. 99**

from the airport and don't expect to be told to have a nice day. Estonia is a strictly no-frills place. If you call a wrong number do not bother to apologise. Just put the phone down. No-one will think you are rude.

One is company, two is a crowd and any more is a

multitude. Estonians don't even live near one another unless they have to. The huge apartment blocks of the Soviet era are a Russian phenomenon, tolerated because of their useful central heating systems and flush toilets. Estonians who can afford it opt for spacious homes so that the occupants need not see one another for days on end, and the big garden will keep a desirable distance between one's own house and one's neighbours. An Estonian probably dreamt up the proverb 'good fences make good neighbours'.

You mind your business and I'll mind mine

Estonian greetings give a good insight into the Estonian mindset. For example, *"Tere tulemast!"* literally means "Hello for coming!" The inclusion of anything like "I'm delighted to see you" or "I've missed you" is a non-starter. Far safer is *"Olete kohale jõudnud"* – "You have arrived." *"Kuidas läheb?"* "How's it going?" is about as warm as an Estonian salutation is likely to be.

> **"You have arrived" or "How's it going?" is about as warm as an Estonian salutation is likely to be.**

This can pose a problem for Estonian subtitlers. Historical costume dramas are prime-time TV viewing but the elaborate courtesy of a Jane Austen or Henry James simply does not exist in minimalist Estonia. *"Astu sisse"* – "Come in" – has to suffice.

Estonians contain their emotions, at least in the presence of outsiders, a state of mind due, in no small measure, to recent Soviet times when a friend of a friend could have informed the KGB about that ill-considered remark you made about the Great Leader whilst under the influence at your cousin's wedding.

Whatever the reason, an Estonian out and about in the world minds his or her own business.

> **❝ Even in an inebriated state most Estonians maintain their reserve. ❞**

The stony veneer may crack when Estonians drink alcohol. Under the influence of strong liquor (and it always is, because Estonians think anything below 20% is a non-alcoholic beverage) your Estonian companions may be seen making strange faces. These grimaces are rudimentary expressions of emotion, and you should also be prepared to contain your amazement if they make a gesture or two. Even in an inebriated state, however, most Estonians maintain their reserve.

The one exception is at the closure of the nation-wide song festival during the singing of the passionately patriotic poem *My County is My Love**, when tearful second and third generations of ex-patriot Estonians embrace their compatriots in an unprecedented display of feeling, and the quarrel over the family pig pen is momentarily forgotten.

* the symbol of resistance and survival, sung from the time when the official national anthem was banned.

Conservatism: "We do it like this"

Estonians are conservative. What was good enough for their mothers and fathers, and the ancestors all the

> **What was good enough for the ancestors all the way back to the Stone Age, is good enough for the modern Estonian.**

way back to the Stone Age, is good enough for the modern Estonian. They will sample *paella*, *sushi* or Irish stew but it is unlikely to become a regular item of their diet. They may even adapt ideas that they see as useful – their love affair with the computer is the most obvious example – but it takes a great deal of time and effort to convince an Estonian to make innovations or change the way that things have always been done. "We do it like this," you see.

Two Estonians, five opinions

When Estonians hanker for a little drama in their lives it can usually be induced by some of the hard stuff. If there are two Estonians, there will be five opinions and several battles of wills. Subject matter is immaterial.

They can talk about impersonal facts till the Baltic cows come home and are long tucked up in their stalls. They can relate details of the Estonian fishing industry. They will enthral you with a description (in a monotone) of the use of oil shale in the power stations. They will effortlessly recount the economic progress of

Mongolia. These are a people who plonked a boulder at the exact mid point of their country (excluding the territory of the islands) – a paragon of accuracy but surely a candidate for the most uninspiring public monument ever.

Discussion of personal, intimate issues is a very different matter. It would be easier to get a computer to cry than to get Estonians to share their innermost feelings, even if they are sharing sheets. A perfect Estonian world would be one in which everybody knew exactly how everybody else felt without ever having to talk about it. You need to understand that Estonians act as if this is already the case.

> **A perfect Estonian world would be one in which everybody knew exactly how everybody else felt without ever having to talk about it.**

In many countries, talking about the weather is used as a way to start lightweight conversation. However, in Estonia if you were to say "It's quite cold today, isn't it?" you could get the reply "I do not agree" or "It was minus 5° Celsius last week, which is 8° Celsius higher than the seasonal average. However, the sea remains frozen near Narva to a depth of approximately 18 centimetres." The only exception to this would be if your host thought you were truly attempting to start a serious debate about cold weather, in which case you might find yourself discussing climate change for the rest of the night.

Common courtesy

On a one-to-one basis, manners can be charming. If an Estonian steps on your foot in the street it is likely that an apology will be swiftly forthcoming and sincere.

Titles are not obligatory as part of a polite introduction. Unlike the Czechs and the Germans, Estonians are indifferent to honours. When you meet someone for the first time it will be a long while before you know if you are talking to an eminent professor or the office cleaner.

A good sign of sprouting friendship is a smile and a double helping of "Hello" – *Tere! Tere!* Green shoots of this kind are worth nurturing for if you can pass the initiation tests (such as sessions in the pub where long silences are an integral part of the proceedings, or the three-year wait for an invitation to somebody's home) that go with getting close to an Estonian, they will be a rock solid friend for life.

> **❝ If you can pass the initiation tests that go with getting close to an Estonian, they will be a rock solid friend for life. ❞**

People use a formal (*teie*) and an informal (*sina*) 'you', but there is no sense of a social gaffe if the *teie–sina* rule is forgotten. Estonians have a similarly light touch with regard to their great and good. Heroes are referred to with a matey familiarity that could shock those nations that are sticklers for protocol, such as the Germans and the Japanese. The esteemed author of the national epic is often affectionately referred to as 'Papa Kreutzwald', for example. A group of Estonian soldiers who returned from the safety of Finland to fight the invading Red Army (at overwhelming odds) in 1944 do not have a grand name such as the 'Noble 600' of the Light Brigade or the 'Coalition of the Willing' – they are simply 'the Finnish lads'.

Everything at the last minute

Estonians live in the here and now. There is no future tense in the Estonian language and Estonian 'plans' for the future, such as they exist at all, are best described as organic.

Whatever an Estonian does it is done without any visible sign of preparation, as if to confuse an invader. If you go to the theatre you may find yourself

> **If you are making a journey with an Estonian, you should be prepared to go at a moment's notice.**

wondering why the auditorium is so empty one minute before the show is set to start when you had always heard that the Estonians are such a cultured bunch. But 20 seconds before curtain up the unruffled Estonians will file in and take their places.

It is the same with travelling. If you are making a journey with an Estonian, you should be prepared to go at a moment's notice. It's take-it-easy or up-and-at-'em with the Estonians and nothing in between.

Conflict

Estonians avoid conflict like the plague. If two people do not get on they feel it's best to avoid one another. An Estonian will always circumnavigate an irredeemably immovable object rather than face it head on, although there could be quite a lengthy discussion and many opinions about the possibilities.

> **66 Speaking one's mind simply reflects a belief that telling the truth cannot be in any way offensive. 99**

Criticism is seldom seen as constructive. It could lead to confrontation and disruption of the quiet deep water of Estonian life.

Causing offence is something an Estonian does by accident, and usually to a foreigner. Estonians are prone to 'telling it like it is'. In Estonia, speaking one's mind simply reflects a belief that telling the truth cannot be in any way offensive. On getting off a train heavily laden, you may well be greeted with "I did not expect you to have so much luggage. My car is small." This can be quite deflating when your suitcases are full of goodies you have brought as presents. Such seeming ungraciousness will soon be overtaken by the successful solving of the logistical problem, and in no time at all your bags will have been accommodated and you will be rattling off down the road with the displaced dog perched on the roof of the car.

Insults are surprisingly tame for a nation that prides

itself on a tough heritage. 'Devil' is about as strong a condemnatory epithet as an Estonian can muster, an indication, if you like, of the spirituality of Estonian life. The weediness of the curse is made up for by frequency of use, usually every other word.

Waste not, want not

Estonians have survived most of their long existence coping with shortages – a shortage of freedom, a shortage of food, a shortage of sun. Add centuries of assorted masters squeezing blood out of the already strained Estonian stone and it's easy to see why they have a deeply frugal attitude to life. Frugality does not extend to hospitality (where the table will be groaning, the welcome will be heartfelt and strong liquor will flow in abundance). You

> **66 Estonians are as sparing with material things as they are with their emotions. 99**

always take something if you are invited to an Estonian home even if it's only a little bunch of wild flowers. *"Tühja käega ära tule!"* – "Don't come with empty hands!" – is not so much an admonition but a reminder of when Estonians were so poor they could not afford enough to go round.

Estonians are as sparing with material things as they are with their emotions. They will use five spoonfuls of coffee to make six cups, save the car battery lights by indicating at the last minute, stand up in the bus to save wear on the seat of trousers, and divide a one-ply serviette in two.

Home & Family

In tune with the natural rhythm of life

Life in Estonia is determined by the seasons. An Estonian firmly believes that to everything there is a season. Spring will bring everyone out of doors as soon as the temperature goes above 3°C and the sap rises after the long winter. Gardens and allotments will be dug, excitable cabin-fevered children will be bundled into the car or taken by bus to one's folk in the country a) to get fresh air and b) to get them out from under your feet while you are busy dragging the garden furniture out from the recesses of the shed.

> **Excitable cabin-fevered children will be bundled into the car or taken by bus to one's folk in the country.**

In summer, don't try and do any business because everyone is in the country. The way that Tallinn empties out in August puts Paris to shame.

Autumn is the time for getting back to work and knuckling down. Parents return to the office and the children to school – an important occasion with the

Estonian tricolour on display outside every home and a lecture from the President. There will be periodic sorties to the forests, headed by an elder who knows all there is to know about fungi, poisonous or otherwise, followed by a feverish round of mushroom and pumpkin pickling and jam making.

> **Home is an idyllic place in which Estonians live in the lull before the ever-expected storm.**

Winter ends the year with deep peace and quiet. Families brave the snow and darkness to gather for the winter solstice. The nation probably owes its current existence to the fact that, in 1991, the USSR tried to invade in the summer – rather than winter, when everyone is hibernating.

No place like home

The Estonian love of home is palpable and potent. Home is an idyllic place in which Estonians live in the lull before the ever-expected storm.

An Estonian home is neat and comfortable. Polished wooden floors give off a comforting gleam and are practical in view of the climate. Estonia is situated at the tip of the Arctic tundra, and winter is mucky as well as inhospitable. This is especially so in March when snow has ceased to be white, fluffy and attractive and has turned to a cloying consistency that clings to the feet and cannot be entirely stamped off on the obligatory mat stationed outside every front door. Summer is a bit better but not much because city pavements are dirty and country roads and paths are covered in a fine layer of dust. Add to this the likelihood of muddy deposits when it rains. Which is often.

> **If you've forgotten your slippers, there's usually a spare pair around that Uncle Tõnu was given as a freebie.**

Shoes, boots, sandals, flip flops must be removed in the entrance hall that will already be festooned with the incumbent family's footwear. Estonians won't care if you have holes in your socks when you visit, and anyway, if you've forgotten your slippers, there's usually a spare pair around that Uncle Tõnu was given as a freebie on a business trip to Helsinki five years ago.

The Family

Estonians are clannish. Family is important. In the Soviet time, fear of the secret police brought kin closer together than in freer, democratic societies. Family members were trusted, strangers were not, and even then one could never be 100% sure. After independence in 1991, families who had been separated for decades greeted one another as if they had parted yesterday and resumed familial bliss or bickering just where they had left off when refugees left in droves in 1944. The process will swing into action whenever there is a family reunion. Returnees can be assured of a warm welcome and be just as sure that the minutiae of ancient feuds are alive and well, and, what is more, stoked by the opportunity to mull them over.

Gender relationships

If there is a little of the Son of Kalev in every Estonian man, luckily there is a little of the Daughter of Linda, SOK's mighty mother, in every Estonian woman. There has to be, because statistics do not paint a rosy picture of the situation for the fairer sex: Estonian women earn 40% less than men for the same jobs.

It's not much better in the romance department. Flowers and candle-lit dinners may be *de rigueur* for an ardent Frenchman and a serenade beneath a window may suit a Latin lover, but a maiden wooed by an Estonian will probably be proffered a bottle of beer. She will have to remove the cap with her teeth, pay for the petrol, drive the boyfriend home after a date and look after the resultant off-spring on her own for the next 20 years. Modern Estonian women, beautiful enough to take their pick, are casting glances further afield now that the EU has opened up the market in eligible chaps.

> **" A serenade beneath a window may suit a Latin lover, but a maiden wooed by an Estonian will probably be proffered a bottle of beer. "**

The elderly

Those who survive into old age and dodge the vicissitudes of Estonian weather and history deserve respect and get it. Pensioners are, for instance, always introduced first and placed at the head of the table for family feasts. Disapproval awaits anyone who raises their shot glass before the presiding elder is ready.

Modern Estonian elders are tough and angry. A hard life has been topped by stingy pensions, rising prices and expensive heath care. They do not understand why bread is dearer now (it is, after all, made of exactly the same ingredients) and having a choice of sausage is deemed unnecessary as they only want the one they have eaten all their lives.

> **66 Disapproval awaits anyone who raises their shot glass before the presiding elder is ready. 99**

The elderly are one of the most ferocious lobby groups in the country and the scourge of gum-chewing youth. Anyone under forty who pushes grandpa aside when exiting the bus will risk being chased down the road dodging blows from a Zimmer frame.

Estonia has few care homes because it's just not done to put old folk 'away'. They wouldn't go anyway. This means that grey power is at its most potent in the home where the elderly can enjoy wide latitude in setting their own agenda. One such, known by the whole family as Auntie Alma and in her late 70s, used to play cards every Sunday with the youngsters of the household. Whenever they played, she would alter the rules to ensure that she would win. This wasn't just tolerated: it was regarded as her right. When she died, it was realised that nobody actually knew the proper version of the rules, and thus the game went with her to the grave.

The young

Estonian children are the nation's treasure. Folk tales are awash with stories of youngsters who are practically swaddled to death. These days the emphasis is on the health-enhancing qualities of fresh air. Babies are still encased in multiple layers to the point of stifling but they are taken out regularly in prams or parked on the veranda of high rise flats in sub-zero temperatures. Many of the layers are retained in summer

> **66 Nanny-ing is not the norm. An Estonian child is expected to work. 99**

because the hope of the nation must be protected not just from sudden gusts of cold air but from the hoards of mosquitoes that emerge from the numerous swamps and bogs (there's always a bog or a swamp nearby: fly swatters are kept at home in handy positions).

Nanny-ing is not the norm. An Estonian child is

expected to work: boys must help dad on the allotment or on the farm, girls must help mother about the house. All must work on school tasks and students must work during university breaks to earn money to supplement their grants.

Parenting style is watchful and affectionate but not sentimental. This means sighing a lot with that formal Estonian exhalation of breath, and giving lectures.

An Estonian child is the recipient of a lot of lectures. The subject can be anything under the sun: the dangers of playing with bare electric wires in Soviet-era derelict factories; the risks of running across thin ice in the spring; the possible consequences of poking the neighbour's pet wolf with a stick.

> **66 Parenting style is watchful and affectionate but not sentimental. This means sighing a lot and giving lectures. 99**

Estonian children are culturally programmed to listen respectfully to their elders' sermons and then go out and do the very thing they've been told not to do. Every day, Estonian children are getting themselves electrocuted and falling through thin ice and being bitten by wolves. The difference is that, unlike most others, the child will make a mental note to convey the same wisdom to his or her offspring in 20 years' time (because "we do it like this"). Thus a perfectly balanced element of Estonian domestic tradition is sustained.

Neighbours

There are only two sorts of Estonian neighbours. Angels or demons. There is no easily understood reason for this. It's not as if there isn't enough room for everyone to live at a reasonable distance from one another. The density of the population is 30 people per square kilometre (compared with, say, the built-up UK at 259 per square kilometre).

Estonian life and literature are littered with pestiferous neighbours who spend their lives either in a state of perpetual envy or plotting how to make mischief. They are like summer

> **66 Estonian life and literature are littered with pestiferous neighbours who spend their lives plotting how to make mischief. 99**

mosquitoes buzzing around performing a plethora of irritating acts from placing their garden fence half a centimetre into your territory, to breaking the dam on which you have laboured long and hard to keep out the ever encroaching swamp. A city equivalent would be letting their dog relieve itself on your carefully cultivated vegetable patch lovingly reclaimed from the urban wasteland. Such neighbours turn up at your funeral looking sorry but, of course, it is far too late by then to make amends.

Angel neighbours help with the garden, bring you home-made jam, tell you when you've left the car lights on, pet sit, and share a bottle of booze at the weekend.

Animals

Many Estonians have a great affinity for their fellow critters, wild or domestic. Bears, lynxes, wolves and elk still inhabit the forests and wild places of the Estonian countryside.

One of the nation's most watched shows is a live relay from a forest glade transmitted via the Internet.

> **One of the nation's most watched shows is a live relay from a forest glade. The stars are wild pigs.**

The stars are wild pigs. Nothing happens for hours on end and when the obliging swine eventually show up for the food that is left for them, excited Estonians call their family and friends at ungodly hours so that they can watch (and hear) the porcine population pigging out. The pigs even get a visit from Old Yuletide, a.k.a. Father Christmas. This concern for wildlife does not, however, stretch to sentimentality. If a wolf should happen by and attack the pigs, they are on their own.

Domestic animals come in two sorts – workers and pets. The working kind have a very belt and braces existence and are expected to earn their keep as guard dogs, rat cats, ornamental pub fish, etc. A 'pet' in Estonian is a *lemmikloom* 'favourite animal' and is very much part of the family. A *lemmikloom* is usually a dog. A German shepherd to be precise – or part thereof. But there is also a trend amongst the up-and-coming middle classes for exotica. A famous artist is known to live in Tartu with his three piranhas, Kurt, Joachim and Herbert.

Lemmikloom deaths are deeply mourned and a family can be incapacitated with grief for weeks. When Arthur, a popular marmalade cat TV celebrity, died aged 14 his show carried on for four years to allow Estonian children to recover from their desolation. Cats whose elderly owners have died retire to the wood shed where they are fed on a regular basis by angel neighbours.

Beliefs & Values

What goes around …

The Estonian philosophy with regard to human nature is determinist. You are what you are and nothing can or should be done to change it. It's a mental approach induced by centuries of powerlessness in their national history, and it has given rise to the concept of *Kahjurõõm* (pronounced 'car-you-rerm') which is (roughly) Estonian for 'sorrow-joy'.

The belief is that what goes around, comes around and it is Fate, not you, that settles the score. (It is

> 66 The belief is that what goes around, comes around. 99

imperative that there is no intervention on your part – a vendetta-type scenario is not at all appropriate. Punishment is earned by the evil-doer. Destiny balances

33

the books.) *Kahjurõõm* refers to the satisfaction of seeing someone who has acted badly towards you come to grief themselves: for example, if a person stole your car only to crash at the end of the street because the steering wheel came off.

Religion: The Pagans

Estonians are, essentially, pantheists. They worship nature – which is just as well because there is a lot of it in Estonia, much of it both primæval and unspoilt. Nearly 50% is forest, and 22% is marshland and bog with a few towns teetering on the edges.

> 66 Estonians worship nature which is just as well because there is a lot of it. 99

Estonians are at ease with nature and treat it with respect. Trees are revered. Echoes of this reverence are everywhere. Road signs are just as likely to direct the curious to the local *hiis* (sacred grove) or even a venerable tree in solitary splendour on a hill as to a castle or manor house. One such tree, the Tamme-Lauri – a sacred oak featured on the Estonian 10 Kroon (EEK) currency – is the oldest and widest tree in Estonia. Seven people could stand inside it before, for safety's sake, it had to be filled in. Every locale can boast a similar spot where, in Spring, trees are decorated with tea lights and festooned with ribbons.

As soon as the spring thaw sets in, the towns are

deserted by early Friday evening. The inhabitants have gone to the country to enact thinly disguised ancient pagan rituals. Fires are lit on sacred rocks by sacred streams, pork is roasted on a sacred fire (barbeque) and fire-water (vodka) is consumed as Estonians carry on in the same time-honoured way as their ancestors. There is even a hard core of official pagans – the *Taara usk*, the faith of Thor or 'Earth believers' – who have a Buddhist-like reverence for life, and believe that everything has a soul, even the ornamental rock in the fish tank.

> 66 Even the trendiest of city folk can be depended on to have a talisman. 99

Not surprisingly, a tradition of *noed* (folk healers) is very much alive; indeed, 50% of the population believe in white witchcraft and will go to the *noed* to cure disease or for remedies for worries untreatable by a modern polyclinic. In their homes, even the trendiest of city folk can be depended on to have a talisman.

Religion: The Christians

Despite a plethora of religions, big and small, from Lutheran Protestantism to paganism, from Buddhism to agnosticism, Estonians – together with Czechs – are the least religious people in the EU.

Christianity, the religion of the invaders, sits uneasily upon the populace. Pastors were complaining well into the 19th century that Estonians treated the church as a social club (too much booze and bagpipes) rather than a place of piety and instruction.

Despite 700 years of Christian missionary work by Germans, Danes and Swedes, statistics do not reveal any significant progress. A poll showed that 16% of Estonians believe in a god (but not any particular one and certainly not one with a capital letter), 54% believe there is some sort of spirit or life force (in line with ancient animistic belief) and 26% are atheist.

In 1992 the parliamentary majority in Estonia's brand new democracy introduced Christian prayers before sessions, but this move was strongly opposed as an attack on freedom of conscience. Some elected representatives lit a sacred fire in a sacred parliamentary waste paper bin then danced around it hooting. The prayers were dropped.

66 Despite 700 years of Christian missionary work, statistics do not reveal any significant progress. 99

Generally, Estonians are curious about religion – the Koran was the top selling book of 2008 – and tolerant of diversity. An Estonian can change religions as others might change coats. During the late 19th century, while under Russian rule, it was thought that conversion to the 'Tsar's faith' would bring favour, and more importantly, land. Thousands became 'born again' Russian Orthodox Christians overnight, and to this day it is Estonia's second largest Christian faith.

Class

There is no class distinction in Estonia. All Estonians were downtrodden for centuries and just as class began to blossom, it was snuffed out by the Communists.

There is no social stigma attached to a regional accent. Dialects are celebrated at the highest level. The President wears a folk costume and quotes long swathes of

> 66 An Estonian who aped the manners and dress of his or her betters was called a 'Juniper German' (juniper bushes have shallow roots). 99

folksy poetry and song in official speeches. Estonians have always mocked those who aspire to be snooty. In the 19th century, an Estonian who aped the manners and dress of his or her betters was called a 'Juniper German' (juniper bushes have shallow roots), a 'willow Russian' (always bowing and scraping) or a 'brush-wood Englishman' (a branch broken off the tree) by the hoi-polloi they tried to leave behind. Whether or not the egalitarian status quo will withstand the test of time is a matter of '*ootame, vaatame*'.

Wealth and Success

Inordinately wealthy Estonians are few and flashy: 30% of the country's wealth is owned by 10% of the population. If you've got it, flaunt it and the more, the better. A big house (American ranch style), a big car (preferably a Hummer), designer clothes and expensive sun specs are essential to trumpet *nouveau-riche* status. Quite whom this ostentation is meant to impress is difficult to fathom. A particularly showy estate near Tallinn is known locally as 'the village of fools'.

Estonia is so small that anyone famous is known to all. A star can be assured that someone can produce a jolly snap taken during potty training or of the famous face in its teenage acne phase. Estonians are not impressed by celebrity. Stars and international super-stars are all very well, but they don't actually do anything useful, such as create outhouses.

Obsessions

Obsession is not a natural part of the usually laid-back national character but there are certain topics guaranteed to awake the Estonians from their 'normal' torpor.

Liberty

An Estonian values liberty above all else. The theme of freedom is at the heart of many an Estonian song, poem, novel, play and film. This is why they never cease to remind visitors of their independent status in rather the same way an elderly person will persist in telling you repeatedly he's still got all his own teeth.

My country

From their little orchids to a brand new Tallinn hotel Estonians cherish anything Estonian. There's even an attachment to a primæval mollusc, an endangered (and protected) bivalve called the freshwater pearl mussel. It is typically Estonian for it spends most of its life calmly and quietly with its bottom stuck in river sediment. If undisturbed, the mussel can live for a century, or even two, and Estonians think it would be nice if the Estonian nation could too.

> **Estonians have the memory of an elephant and they never forget their forebears.**

The Estonians know they are a small nation and cut their coat according to their cloth. The social activist and folklorist pastor Jakob Hurt encouraged Estonians to 'be great in spirit', doubting that the neighbours would let them be anything else.

Monument mania

Estonians have the memory of an elephant and they never forget their forebears. All monuments to the fallen of the War of Independence were destroyed by the Soviets. These have been replaced, and new ones added at a rate of knots, in a drive that amounts to obsession. You don't have to be an Estonian or 'great' to get one. There's a memorial in Tallinn to Britain's Michael 'Beef' Park, co-driver of Estonian rally ace

Markko Märtin.

You don't even have to be a person. There is a monument for the Russian Rouble (1940-1992) cheering the passing of Lenin from the currency, and one to the Estonian language that celebrates the 'Mother Tongue'.

Owning a car

A small, rich minority own showy cars, but for the average Estonian, a car means something much more important than status, it means freedom. To the young it is the equivalent of a Viking galley, enabling travel and adventure. To the family it may mean convenience and comfort in a village where the bus comes twice a day on workdays and not at all at weekends.

> **For the average Estonian, a car means something much more important than status, it means freedom.**

Some 60% of cars in Estonia are more than 10 years old. So, while it may be a BMW, it's an old BMW. But old is not a problem. An elderly car, the pride and joy of its owner, will be lovingly washed on the driveway, and when the old machine finally gives up the ghost it will not go to the breaker's yard. Its final resting place will be the garden of its home where the next generation can drive it along imaginary highways and it can relive the purring shiny days of its youth. All things, inanimate as well as animate, have souls.

Security

A Soviet habit of descending on people to arrest them in the middle of the night has bred in the Estonians a passion for extreme security measures. The locks and bolts on their gates and doors would do justice to Fort Knox. When visiting an Estonian home you should expect a protracted period before you can actually enter. You will have to wait at the electronically operated front gate and, if it's dark, tolerate being dazzled by a sudden illumination of bright

> **66 The locks and bolts on Estonian gates and doors would do justice to Fort Knox. 99**

lights. Having avoided the guard dog inside the gate and safely negotiated the path, there will be another pause outside the front door while those inside peer at you through the spy hole or the security camera whilst addressing you suspiciously through the intercom. Another interval will ensue while the Yale and mortice locks and an assortment of bolts are undone.

Security firms (complete with smart uniformed guards and packs of slavering German shepherds or Rottweilers) are some of the most successful businesses in Estonia.

Grooming and beauty

Estonians take a pride in their appearance. Even those with worn clothes artfully mended will examine themselves in the mirror in the hall, use a clothes brush and comb their hair to make sure they are properly groomed before going anywhere, even if it's just to the corner shop.

It is important to have the right kit – smart clothes for the opera, padded jackets for skiing, Lycra shorts for cycling. Hard hats on building sites are worn not so much for seldom-heeded health and safety regulations but to show that the wearer knows the correct dress code.

> **❝ It is important to have the right kit – smart clothes for the opera, Lycra shorts for cycling. ❞**

An extension of careful grooming is the obsession with beauty. Every other shop is an *ilusalong* – a beauty salon. Glamour goods – lingerie, cosmetics, haute couture – and cosmetic surgery reached Estonia only latterly, and the beauty industry has exploded.

One reason for this is Carmen Kass, supermodel for Dior, Victoria's Secret and Max Factor, President of the Estonian Chess League and one of the world's most visible Estonians. Beauty contests, glossy women's magazines, and TV programmes about the fashion industry enhance the fairy tale. Every girl dreams of being discovered, like Kass, by a modelling scout in a supermarket whilst rummaging around in the cold cabinet for grannie's sausage of choice.

Singing

Estonians have been enthusiastic singers since time out of mind. Singing is not just a national hobby – it's an Estonian trademark. Every town and village has its own singing ground, *lauluvaljak*, and you don't have to go far anywhere before you hear some sort of trilling, be it the library, the park or the pub.

The five-yearly All-Estonia Song Party (*laulupidu* – literally 'singing party') is the only time the Estonians make a great deal of noise, with choirs 20,000 strong – all impeccably attired in regional costumes – and audiences five or six times that number.

If you are on a bus or a tram in the centre of Tallinn on the day the *laulupidu* comes to town, you will be held up by a long procession with flags flying and brass bands playing, and crowds of people (many hanging out of windows and perched in trees) cheering them on.

This is a big festival, with dance troupes as well as choirs. In the week before the event Estonian tribes, both local and international, begin

> **Singing is not just a national hobby – it's an Estonian trademark. Every town and village has its own singing ground.**

to gather. Towns such as Toronto, Canada, Sydney, Australia and Portland, Ohio, USA become a whit depleted as their denizens, national costumes neatly folded in flight bags, head off for the ritual pilgrimage to their ancestral homelands and spiritual Mecca.

Most will stay in hotels because, although they love Estonia with all their heart and soul, they are not always so keen on their relations. In any case some, particularly the Americans and Canadians, are less than enthusiastic about the outhouse on the family farm.

> **For two days the Estonians and their brothers and sisters from around the globe sing their socks off in an orgy of folk karaoke.**

For two days the Estonians and their brothers and sisters from around the globe sing their socks off in an orgy of folk karaoke liberally aided by lashings of drink. Then, almost as soon as the last note of the current bash has faded away and the Olympic-style flame or 'sun-fire' in the stadium is extinguished, the choirs and dance troupes hop into their buses, trains and planes to return from whence they came – to begin beavering away at rehearsals for the next time. Until then there will be constant re-runs on TV. If you are back home in Canada, you can relive the great day with snippets on YouTube.

Punks have their own *Punklaulupidu* (Punk song festival) attended by the President and broadcast on national TV, alongside bands such as Guiltless Grannie and Smoke Stinking Singer.

Punks enjoy national admiration because in 1988, when their Western equivalents were urinating on the Union Jack or the Stars and Stripes, they were shinning up the tower of the Tallinn stadium's song bowl to replace the Communist red flag with the nation's tricolour of blue, black and white.

Leisure & Pleasure

Sauna and spas

Estonians believe that rest and relaxation are as essential for their well being as pills and surgery.

Natural mineral waters and therapeutic mud are abundant in Estonia and their curative power has long been known to folk medicine. Purpose-built spas started to appear in the late 1800s to treat the indolent rich of nearby St. Petersburg. Today, it's normal to be found chilling out in brown stuff or covered in sticky honey awaiting a massage.

The sauna in traditional society was a mini health and hygiene centre where Estonians witnessed the beginning, the middle and the end of their lives. It was not only the washhouse and the place where bacon was smoked and cured, but also where brides were ceremoniously washed, where women gave birth and where the dying made their final bed. By contrast, today's sauna is 20% about washing and 80% about networking; so, if you want to conduct serious business, the sauna is the place to do it.

> **66 Estonians believe that rest and relaxation are as essential for their well being as pills and surgery. 99**

The traditional location for a sauna is in the middle of a field in the country where, having heated a small wooden room to a minimum of 70-80°C (160-180 °F), you spend the requisite amount of broiling to work up a complexion worthy of a lobster and,

> **Lashing your body with a 'whisk' of fragrant birch twigs is optional, but they must be fresh or the leaves will stick to your skin.**

after the equally requisite swig of the national tipple, jump into a nearby pond. Lashing your body with a 'whisk' of fragrant birch twigs is optional, but they must be fresh otherwise the leaves will stick to your skin and you'll be doing a passable imitation of a tree. The following joke gives an idea of how Estonians like their sauna:

> An Estonian is captured by cannibals who put him into a cooking pot and clamp down the lid. After half an hour the lid is taken off. The cannibals find the Estonian in relaxed mood and requesting another log on the fire.

Estonians are completely unselfconscious about their bodies. Sauna is often a social occasion and one is expected to enter nude. In some households one shares the sauna with others nude regardless of gender and a post-sauna towel would be treated as a sign of eccentricity.

No Estonian could imagine life without the sauna.

Anything less than a weekly session is unthinkable. To relax in the sauna is, as always with Estonians, deeply practical as well as a pleasure. An old folk saying goes: 'If booze or the sauna won't help, the illness is fatal.'

Sex

Estonians are not prudish about sexual matters. Hardcore porn magazines in the supermarket are on the same shelves as children's magazines.

Relationships are no-frills. No surprise there, then. The genderless, status-less, Estonian word for co-habitee, husband or wife, is *abielu* – 'help in life', a straightforward job description of what is expected of an Estonian partner. An anecdote tells of a man whose wife was unfaithful. She was a most attractive woman and had many lovers. A friend advised the man to get a divorce but he was not interested. "What for?" he asked, "I would only have to join the queue."

> **The genderless, status-less, Estonian word for co-habitee, husband or wife, is *abielu* – 'help in life'.**

Going spare

Estonians love to make something from nothing. If an article really cannot be resuscitated (the damage must be terminal), Estonians show remarkable expertise in 'recycling'. They regard it as natural to re-use just about anything. If they have a broken fridge, they will tinker with it, and next time you're round it will have been repainted and redeployed as a bookshelf, or a kennel for the dog.

The idea of clearing out junk from the house would be akin to taking one's birthright to the tip. Holding on to everything you ever owned is a national pastime.

Swinging

Every Estonian village has a giant wooden swing – a *kiik*. This is always big enough to accommodate at least four adults standing up. If this sounds tame, then you are encouraged to try the *kiiking* that involves being clamped to the seat of a swing by your feet and working your way up to a stomach-churning 360° circle at high speed.

The small outdoors

Lucky Estonians own a summer cottage – *suvila* – where the family spends as much time as possible as soon as the weather is good enough to get their jalopy down the dirt track. Others share a patch of nature, even if it is on a bit of wasteland between the tower blocks on a Soviet-era urban housing estate. Little kitchen allotments and flower gardens can be found nestling in the most unlikely spots.

Supplementary to many houses or *suvila*-s is the

'yard' where animals can be kept, a garden cultivated by the women, and where the men lurk in the tool shed, smoking, drinking, distilling alcohol and doing crosswords by the light of a lamp lit by an ingeniously laid-on but terrifyingly parlous supply of electricity.

> **66 The men lurk in the tool shed, smoking, drinking, distilling alcohol and doing crosswords. 99**

Entertainment goes outdoors in summer. A ruined castle, a picturesque lake dotted with giant floating candles, the seashore, an ancient hill fort – all become the settings for plays, music and poetry. The shows go on regardless of weather, so a necessary adjunct to your evening dress is a cheap, transparent plastic rain cape.

Sport: the Kalev connection

Sport is popular, and it shows when the Estonians do surprisingly well, for such a tiny country, at the Olympic Games.

Football has a big following, but mostly from an armchair with a can of beer in hand. No-one expects the Estonian national team to win any cups but the game is still followed with (for Estonians) a great deal of emotion – meaning a solitary squawk of "*urra*" when the home team score an unexpected goal.

Estonians admire SOK-style physical strength. Even today there are hay-making competitions, where the local lads, using scythes, bare their chests and show off their physical prowess. The gallery of Estonian heavyweights includes Georg Lurich, a wrestler who won international medals for the Tsar and earned pin money as a circus strongman. Another wrestler, Martin Klein, won a silver medal at the 1912 Olympics after a match that lasted eleven hours.

> **"Estonians are the world champions in Wife Carrying. The prize is the wife's weight in beer. "**

But it is Kristjan Palusalu who, for many Estonians, is the most revered heavyweight athlete of all. He won gold at the 1936 Berlin Olympics, but in 1940 was arrested by the Soviets and deported to a hard labour camp. In true SOK style he escaped, was captured, condemned to death, escaped again and came home. His streak of rotten luck continued, for after the second Soviet invasion in 1944 he was imprisoned again. He was eventually released but his career was ruined. He remains a hugely popular hero, perhaps because his life reflected that of the nation.

Estonians are the world champions in Wife Carrying, an international sport with a category in the *Guinness Book of Records*. The prize is the wife's weight in beer. The idea supposedly derived from a Finno-Ugric past in which men courted women by seizing them and carrying them away from their villages. Several types of 'carry' are permissible:

piggyback, fireman's carry (over the shoulder) and the Estonian-style carry where the wife hangs upside-down on her husband's back with her legs around his shoulders, holding onto his waist. The Estonians lost the championship in 2009 (to the Finns) but determined efforts are under way to regain world domination.

> **If you are looking for an evening of sparking wit then it is best to give Estonian comedy a miss.**

The latest, and rather more graceful, sports heroes are cross-country Olympic gold winning skiers Kristina Smigun and Andrus Veerpalu.

The chess master Paul Keres is the sporting hero for more intellectual Estonians. From 1936 to 1965 Keres was among the top ten chess players in the world but, as he always fell a whisker short of the championship, he was known as 'the eternal second'.

Sense of Humour

If you are looking for an evening of sparking wit then it is best to give Estonian comedy a miss. The ingenuous theatrical comedy *What a bumpkin!* – the first original play ever to be written by an Estonian – still represents what constitutes good clean fun of the slipping-on-a-banana-skin sort. In-jokes are popular. One famous novel opens with a peasant returning from the manor groaning in agony and blaming a cake. Any Estonian would assume that he has been beaten for scoffing the baron's food, but it turns out that the 'cake' the dimwit has eaten is soap. This type of localised humour can be impenetrable to outsiders.

> **Despite the often stony face that Estonians choose to present to the world at large, self-parody is common.**

Despite the often stony face that Estonians choose to present to the world at large, self-parody is common and in-house jokes about Estonian slowness are legion.

For example:

A UFO floated above Tallinn for five hours: two Estonians caught the moment and got some snaps.

Snails are very expensive in Estonia because there are only a few people fast enough to catch them.

The Estonians got back at the Soviet Russians by ridiculing them behind their backs. For example:

Ivan and Peter were staring up a flagpole, scratching their heads. An old farmer driving by stopped to ask: "What's the problem, comrades?" Peter answers: "The foreman wanted us to measure the height of the flag pole, but it's too skinny to climb." The farmer goes to his truck and brings back a monkey wrench and a measuring tape. He loosens a couple of bolts, lowers the pole to the ground, then measures it. "Seven and a half metres, comrades" then takes his stuff and drives on. Ivan looks at Peter and chuckles: "A muck spreader if I ever saw one. We wanted the height, and he gives us the length."

Estonian children swap jokes about the young smart-ass, Juku, e.g:

Juku is walking down the street. Suddenly a tramp jumps on him and says "100 kroon or your life", Juku gives the tramp money saying "Here's 50 kroon, you've already frightened me half to death."

Teacher to Juku's mother: "Your son is so thirsty for knowledge! Who does he get it from?"
"The knowledge from me, the thirst from his father."

Only a few Estonians find Estonian humour funny, and even then they make no effort to look as if they're actually enjoying themselves. In the unlikely event of their being persuaded to tell a joke of their own, you must watch the speaker carefully so that you can spot when it's over. This takes practice as it is often not at all obvious when this point has been reached. A good guideline is to laugh politely after the

> **66** Only a few Estonians find Estonian humour funny, and even then they make no effort to look as if they're actually enjoying themselves. **99**

speaker has been silent for several minutes. If you are worried about whether to laugh or not, don't laugh. Always remember that there is no observable difference between the behaviour of an Estonian who has enjoyed a joke, and a visitor who doesn't realise he has just heard one.

Culture

Estonian fine arts are characterised by brevity. Reflecting the paucity of resources that Estonians have always lived with, no more musical notes, brush strokes or words are used than is necessary to convey the point. This sparseness says more about what an Estonian sees and feels than any words could.

Fantastical fantasies

The Estonian imagination is a powerful instrument powered by dreaming for centuries about a better lot.

66 The national epic set a pattern of disguising serious subject matter in myth and fantasy. 99

The national epic set a pattern of disguising serious subject matter (in this case the hidden history of the Estonian people) in myth and fantasy. Written in the mid 1800s, *SOK* got past the Russian censor by being presented as a quaint example of the oral tradition of an interesting but expiring sub-species. The Estonians, however, knew better and, looking under the surface, recognised and cherished the depiction of the 'ancient fight for freedom' – the struggles of the ancestors against the crusaders.

Apart from dodging the censor, the author, Dr. Friedrich R. Kreutzwald, had a tricky job on his hands adapting earthy tales heard in his country surgery to suit the delicate sensibilities of the 19th century. Before being re-cast as a heroic king, the oversized, nameless (like the Estonia of its time) Son of Kalev was violent and aggressive (as northern trolls tend to be), with a very unprogressive attitude to women.

> **6 The original tale had our hero being grabbed by the testicles and thrown into a swamp by Jesus. 9**

The original tale had our hero being grabbed by the testicles and thrown into a swamp by Jesus. So annoying were the irrepressible giant's antics that Jesus finally threw him into hell, whence SOK was last seen gaily waving goodbye. Jesus does not make an appearance in Kreutzwald's epic (unlike its prototype the Finnish *Kalevala*). On the contrary, its pages are littered with pre-Christian imps and devils.

Satan pops up often in Estonia, be it in a homely performance in a barn by a 'farm theatre' or leaping around the stage of the national ballet in the capital city. His many guises include *Vanapagan* (literally 'the old pagan'), a big, amiable simpleton; 'The Black Gentleman', looking uncannily like a German parson; a Hellenic northern faun grazing berries in the forest; and the patient, good-natured and put-upon tenant of a run-down farm in the work by Anton Hansen Tammsaare (the greatest 20th-century Estonian prose writer), *The new old pagan of Hellbottom Farm*.

> **❝ Superman is invited to Estonia to rescue a damsel in distress and gets accidentally drunk on day one at a song festival. So the damsel has to be rescued by swallows... ❞**

Fantasy is still alive and well in tales by the popular contemporary author, Andrus Kivirähk. In one story, Superman is invited to Estonia to rescue a damsel in distress and gets accidentally drunk (he can't take strong liquor) on day one at a song festival. So the damsel has to be rescued by swallows, three blue lions (Estonia's national symbols) and a drunken, pot-bellied middle-aged Estonian.

Music

As one would expect from a nation that expresses itself so copiously and ardently in music, the most famous Estonian in the world today is probably the composer, Arvo Pärt, with the Järvi family of conductors not far behind.

Talking (reluctantly) about his minimalist compositions Pärt expresses the great Estonian yearning for paring things down: "The complex and many-faceted only confuses me, and I must search for unity. What is it, this one thing, and how do I find my way to it?" This statement reflects the same spirit as that of an Estonian scientist who dismissed 'too much information' in his research. Many of Pärt's slow, meditative scores evoke sadness, resolve and quiet hope, and capture not a little of the essence of the Estonian soul.

> **Many of Pärt's slow, meditative scores evoke sadness, resolve and quiet hope, and capture not a little of the essence of the Estonian soul.**

Singing is ubiquitous but brass band music is also widely played. This is a leftover from the days when the non-conformist church was a force in the land and Estonian lay preachers were translating *Pilgrim's Progress* for surreptitious circulation under the noses of the Tsarina's secret police. Whilst the Christian message has not been an overwhelming hit, Methodist music has. John Wesley was of the opinion that the devil should not have all the best tunes, and who better to show this off with a vengeance than a motley crew of enthusiastic amateur musicians, music in one hand, brightly polished instrument in the other, blasting their way through *Lucky Lips* at the head of a column wending its way to the local song festival ground.

Films

Classic films are aired time and again on TV on special days. Repetition is not a problem for Estonians. Much loved and often cited as the number one choice of all films is *Spring, Kevade*, from the book by Oskar Luts. Many regard Luts' novel as the repository of everyday 'normal' Estonian-ness as opposed to the saga of the mythological SOK. The book is based on the author's schooldays in the early 1900s in a village near Tartu – the first about such a subject in Estonian literature. Every man, woman and child can recite the opening line and is familiar with the rich, robust, Dickensian gallery of characters. The charm of the film is enhanced by the fact that the parts were played not by actors but by ordinary children who, as they grew up, repeated their smash hit roles in *Summer, Suvi* (1976) and *Autumn, Sügis* (1990).

> **The cast of infant-eating goblins who live in dark forests beside deep, bleak lakes could come as a shock.**

The film adaptation of another Oskar Luts book *The Little Imp* is also a regular. The roots of *The Little Imp* are much older than *Spring* and, despite being made for children, the film is a veritable banquet for ethnologists. Apart from its lyrical musical score, the cast of infant-eating goblins who live in dark forests beside deep, bleak lakes could come as a shock to a child brought up in the protected, rarefied culture of My Little Pony.

The last in a trilogy of perennial favourites is the cult film *The Last Relic*. Set in the Livonian War of the 16th century but really about getting out from under the Soviet yoke, it's a love story starring a box of bones.

Television

95% of Estonians have television and 51% are able to receive international programmes by cable. Estonians watch a lot of TV: the same chilly weather factor that encourages the use of mobile phones and the Internet combines with frugality (there is no Estonian TV licence fee) to produce a nation of telly addicts. The news is watched obsessively to check if there is an invader on the way.

Children's television is charming and witty. and full of a love of nature and animals: local characters include The Wolf with Shifty Eyes and the Mommi Bear family. Finnish Moomins and the Swedish Pippi Longstocking ("I like to do things by myself") reinforce the Scandinavian connection.

> **66 Children's television is charming and witty: local characters include The Wolf with Shifty Eyes. 99**

From the colourful, clever cartoon serial created by Eesti Joonisfilm (the only animation studio in eastern Europe to survive the ending of Soviet subsidies) comes Lotte the puppy and her friends. You can meet them in person on the last day of school when children are allowed to wear what they please and the order of the day is fancy dress.

Estonians love soap operas and a cornucopia of cheap and cheerful foreign productions is on offer. *Wildcat, The Bold and the Beautiful, Stormy Passion*, etc., feature Latin excesses acted out with the original dialogue turned down and a monotonous simultaneous translation in Estonian (for those who can't read fast enough to keep up with the action) superimposed.

> **66 It's wise to avoid visiting anyone when the local soaps are broadcast. Even the little conversation you may have expected will completely dry up. 99**

It's wise to avoid visiting anyone when the local soaps such as *The home in the middle of town* and *13 Happiness Street* are broadcast. Even the little conversation you may have expected will completely dry up until the last credit has dropped off the screen.

Strong stomachs are needed for Estonian documentaries about cops and ambulance teams on the job because they show uncensored real events, and each episode features injuries, corpses and litres of blood in sordid detail and remorseless close up. Emergency services are called *kiirabi* – 'quick help' in Estonian.

Chat shows have never got off the ground since normal Estonian reticence and conservatism are not the stuff that successful chat shows are made of. Many watch *Oprah* on cable if they want a nosy fix on how the other half lives. Estonians love melodrama but like to keep it at a distance. To them it is rather like performing seals at the circus. No-one wants to be like them, but they are fascinating to watch.

Custom & Tradition

Old folks

Folk culture is still a potent force in Estonia. Other nations may have forgotten what a maypole is and be unable to sing traditional nursery rhymes, but any Estonian school child knows a brace of them, plus a heap of songs and poems, and usually has a folk costume at home. Children have a song and dance festival all of their own every five years and it's huge, just like the adult version. The only difference is that booze is not sold inside the festival grounds so the café outside the gate does a roaring trade attending to the needs of thirsty adults.

> 66 If there's a children's singing contest on TV everybody watches, and next day people discuss the event at work. 99

If there's a children's singing contest on TV (different levels and different age grades), everybody watches, and next day people discuss the event at work – even those who don't have children. After all, when it's your family's or your neighbour's child, it has far more pull than the X Factor.

Traditional dress

Estonians do not wear fur or leather. They wear linen or wool. This is because a) fur was a luxury that only the barons (ruling class) could afford, and b) arable and sheep farming, not cattle raising, was the traditional activity of peasant farmers. Cows were kept for small yields of milk and meat but often the most useful bovine by-product was manure for the crops. Woolly sheep fared better in the chilly climate.

Cardigans or pullovers are a must for national dress even on rare occasions when the temperature is +30°, and in winter girls are kitted out in cosy hand-knitted 'bear pants' which are thick and woolly and give them the look of furry cubs when tumbling about in the snow. Some items (a woollen skirt wrapped round the hips fastened with a belt, a woollen shirt-like coat, a linen blouse with sleeves) were worn routinely well into the 19th century and it's the 'Sunday best' versions that have become national costumes. Accessories are handed down from mother to daughter for generations. Jewellery, brooches and the spectacular silver cones (weighing up to 11 kilos) worn on the breasts of the south Estonian Setu tribeswomen are not just for decoration; they are magical talismans to protect the wearer against evil.

❝ In winter girls are kitted out in cosy hand-knitted 'bear pants'. ❞

Belts and mittens were also believed to have potent

protective powers. It's even possible to get a little knitted mobile phone holder with an ancient symbol doubtless concocted in order to repel the mosquitoes of modern life, cold callers.

Everyone wears a hat. Old ladies wear berets or fancy German-style felt hats with feathers. Children wear a *müts* (cap) that comes in a multitude of manifestations from the traditional round linen brimless kind to baseball caps. Crocheted cotton caps are indispensable baby wear.

> **66** Though many Estonians have forgotten their original significance, festivities are closely connected with ancestor worship. **99**

One accessory is essential in winter – a 'sparkler'. Every year around 50 people are killed on unlit roads so from October to April a 'cats-eye' reflector is a legal necessity for pedestrians and cyclists. These come in forms to suit all tastes – plain, dragons, cats, smiley faces, aeroplanes and Estonia-shaped maps. All over the country in winter, they dangle from coats and rucksacks – flashes of bright light in the night.

Magic moments

Though many Estonians have forgotten their original significance, festivities are closely connected with ancestor worship and fertility rites are widely celebrated. Hallowe'en (All Saints' Eve) coincides with the start of the pagan 'Time of Souls' when the dead return. Death, apparently, does little to ameliorate the crusty Estonian character. A visiting spirit has been recorded as complaining volubly that he had been buried in a blue blouse rather than a white one. The 'Time of Souls' has a very upbeat aspect because, if everything has an animus, then objects as well as humans and animals can come back. If you crave a reunion with an item that lingers in your memory, or a favourite tree, then dim the electric lights, take a match to the candle, put out snacks, keep very still (the spirits detest noise) and be patient. Check out the sauna (the favoured revenant venue) every now and then. If you haven't got a sauna, try the shower...

> **66 A visiting spirit has been recorded as complaining volubly that he had been buried in a blue blouse rather than a white one. 99**

The equivalent of American 'trick or treaters' arrive in November. Everyone is a target – great (Parliament gets a visit) or small. Mini-minstrels recite a poem, sing a song or play a tune before they are given sweets, today's substitute for the meat or grain that used to symbolise hoped-for produce.

St. Martin's Day (10th November) is the day to placate the ancestor-guardians of the crops. Minstrels will appear at your front door to wish you good luck. St. Catherine's Day (25th November) is a women's festival and another flotilla takes to the streets to placate the guardians of the cattle.

Shrove Tuesday can only be fêted in the countryside because it is celebrated with a sleigh ride that is meant to ensure a good crop of flax. You can enjoy the last of the snowy forests and fields and, if you are hungry after all that exhilarating fresh air and also want to commune further with the ancestors, get stuck into a traditional helping of bean soup with a pig's foot that will satisfy both needs very nicely.

> **❝ Shrove Tuesday is celebrated with a sleigh ride that is meant to ensure a good crop of flax. ❞**

There are few Estonian households who do not celebrate the summer solstice, the longest day of the year. The 23rd June is the time when the northern 'white nights' reach their apogee and there is hardly any darkness to speak of. Fire comes into its own with a big bonfire containing the collected detritus of the spring months which will burn until dawn, when Dawn and Dusk are said to exchange a brief kiss before parting until the same time next year.

I do and er...thank you

An Estonian wedding is quick, simple and well lubricated. After a straightforward ceremony, often in the tradition of the Lutheran faith, everybody gets merrily tipsy. Indeed, it is common for the gathering (including the pastor) to be fairly well oiled within a few hours of the happy event.

Wedding speeches are almost endearing for their awkwardness. Thus the father of the bride might say something like:

"Ladies and gentlemen, I have known my daughter all her life. Er…, she also has known me for that time. I have known her husband for a shorter period. I will no doubt be seeing more of him in the future, as will my wife – and my daughter. Er…, thank you."

Birthdays and personal anniversaries are not major events. Nor is there a particular duty to celebrate them with family members. It would be quite normal for a man to say to his work colleagues, "Today is my seventh wedding anniversary. Shall we go for a drink?" For the wife to turn up for the start of the evening would be regarded as bad form, but she would be most welcome to come along towards the end of the evening in order to give everyone a lift home.

Quiet Yuletide and Happy New Year!

The most important festival for old Estonians was the winter solstice, Yuletide. Nowadays it is Christmas. Preparations begin on 24th December when the women give the home a good clean while the men stoke the sauna and fetch in a fir tree from the nearby forest. If there isn't a forest handy then the local shopping mall has to do.

The main dish is eaten on Christmas Eve. Estonian families still eat a peasant meal whose centrepiece is sausages made of pigs' blood, barley and morsels of pork smeared with bacon fat and roasted until crackling. This is accompanied by roasted potatoes, hot sauerkraut (not very sour at all) and home-made cranberry jam.

Presents are distributed on Christmas Eve, so parents can indulge themselves as much as they like on the strong, dark porter that

> **66 Celebrations are short, and time off work is usually two or three days – barely enough to recover from the hangover. 99**

breweries produce especially for the season, knowing that the children will not wake them early because Father Christmas has come and gone. This custom is so practical that generations of Estonian migrants around the world continue celebrating on 24th December. Celebrations are short, and time off work is usually limited to two or three days – barely enough to recover from the hangover.

Outdoor electric illuminations have become very popular and the Estonians leave them in place to light up the winter darkness and cheer the hearts and minds of passers-by until well into February when the days start to get longer.

On the last night of the outgoing year – Estonians

don't trust the future so they celebrate the passing of the old one – town squares are packed with people watching a digital countdown whilst texting and chatting on their mobiles and imbibing bottles of Soviet 'champagne', a cheap fizzy white wine that is still very much a part of any Estonian celebration. Singles wishing for coupledom stand a good chance of getting a proposal on 31st December or very early on 1st January – though the risk of 'marry in haste, repent at leisure' is high.

Flag days

Estonians didn't have a flag until the late 19th century and were not allowed to use it for half of the next one, so they now stick it up at the first whiff of a special occasion.

> **66 Estonians didn't have a flag until the late 19th century so they now stick it up at the first whiff of a special occasion. 99**

It is very much in evidence on Independence Day on 24th February and the Restoration of Independence Day on 20th August, which mark the 1918 and 1991 return of liberty (respectively). The country celebrates with official speeches, military parades and, of course, local homespun events that usually involve a song or two and a band. If Estonians could paint a flag big enough to cover the entire country, it would be on these two days.

Other commemorative days include Holocaust Memorial Day at the end of January, Mother Tongue Day in March and Commemoration Day for the victims of World War II in May. Remembrance Day in June is an exclusively local occasion that commemorates the executions and deportations to Siberia (without trial) of up to 110,000 'enemies of the state' (meaning middle-class Estonians) during the Stalinist period. Victory Day on 23rd June celebrates the anniversary of the Battle of Võnnu when a ragamuffin army of Estonians and Latvians thrashed the mighty German Landeswehr in a battle in 1919 that secured the country's first period of independence.

The only thing missing from the list of National Days is Estonian National Days' Day – a tribute to the exhausted organisers who make sure the right flags are flying on the right buildings on the right days. Estonia cannot afford any more dramatic political upheavals lest, to commemorate some event or other, every day becomes a national holiday.

> **The only thing missing from the list of National Days is Estonian National Days' Day – a tribute to the exhausted organisers.**

The dead

Estonians like the dead. They have one attribute that the living cherish – they are silent.

Death is dealt with in a characteristic no-nonsense way, although a funeral is one of the few occasions when people will (discreetly) show their feelings without the ingestion of alcohol. Even if the service is Christian, many of those attending will have come to say farewell forever as the belief in any afterlife is practically non-existent. Tearful mourners file quietly past the open coffin and kiss or caress the deceased who gradually disappears under a blanket of flowers and garlands.

> **The body will be carried by the men of the family to the 'garden of death' on a path strewn with fir sprigs.**

At a traditional village funeral the body will be carried by the men of the family to the 'garden of death' on a path strewn with fir sprigs, the emblem of the spirit of the forest. Many photographs will be taken of both the funeral and the supper that follows so that the solemn occasion may be recalled again (and again). Gravestones are low and unostentatious and are just as likely to have a flame etched into them as a cross.

The 'garden of death' is a haven of peace and tranquillity. Estonians believe one must not disturb or take anything away from cemeteries where the picking of flowers is actually prohibited. Graves are beautifully kept and the neatly tended plots have benches for relatives who come for a wordless chat, usually accompanied by a little libation.

Eating & Drinking

Food

Nothing epitomises the enduring Estonian attachment to peasant values more than their love of hearty, cholesterol-loaded food. Estonians like to eat. They spend 36% of their income on edibles, as opposed to, say, the Czechs, whose equivalent figure is 25%.

Meals are large, both at home and in restaurants. This is partly a reaction to half a century of Soviet scarcity. Having spent years queuing and competing with half the town for a one-off consignment of tins of tuna, Estonians revel in the range of choice.

> **66 It's normal to eat food that has gone off – sour cream, sour cabbage – because *hapu* means both 'sour' and 'pickled'. 99**

Bread is sacrosanct and the rest of the meal is 'something to go with the bread'. Consumption of dairy products and marinated or pickled food is high. An Estonian joke makes fun of the fact that it's normal to eat food that has gone off – sour cream, sour milk, sour cucumber, sour pumpkin, sour cabbage – because *hapu* means both 'sour' and 'pickled'. Jars of assorted preserves, usually home produced, will appear on most tables for most meals, presented in screw-top glass containers of a dazzling variety of shapes and sizes which accumulate in the garden shed and come into their own in the autumn bottling season.

Estonians eat a lot of home-grown fruits and vegetables. Over 20% of their food they either grow or get from friends or relatives. The planting and gathering of produce is a source of great pleasure and any exertions are inevitably followed by a cheerful alcohol-laced party to quench thirsts brought on by unaccustomed and greatly treasured days down on the farm.

❝ Fish is important, but meat is a must. Estonians are convinced carnivores. ❞

Russian influence is seen, or rather smelled, most strongly in summer when *shashlik* – meat (usually pork) on skewers – is grilled in Estonian gardens. Other Russian dishes that form a regular part of the Estonian diet are small portions of meat in pastry parcels called *pelmeni* (the North's answer to ravioli), and *seljanka*, a thick meaty soup (the North's answer to minestrone). Fish is important, but meat is a must. Estonians are convinced carnivores. Vegetarianism is not normal.

Additives considered by many countries to be unhealthy are still the norm in Estonia. People put salt on their food before they've even tried a mouthful. As the cooks will have already added a couple of kilos to the dish, you could float on their soups like the Dead Sea. The vast quantities of salt ingested are matched by truly voluminous amounts of sugar. Estonians have a very sweet tooth and love fancy and dainty cakes (the art of the confectioner is thriving) and would kill for chocolate. Even the hint of a possibility that there could be a salt or sugar shortage is guaranteed to bring out shoppers in droves, with queues at food stores stretching the 185 kilometre (115 miles) distance between Tallinn and Tartu.

Drink

Everybody is thirsty in Estonia, no doubt because of all the salt in the food. While they like to eat, the Estonians love to drink. Ironically, they make fun of their Russian and Finnish neighbours for drinking too much. The Finnish and Estonian languages are very similar, which leads some to say that "Finnish is what Estonian sounds like when you're drunk."

> **Everybody is thirsty in Estonia, no doubt because of all the salt in the food.**

Heavy drinking is widespread but performs an essential function – it allows the Estonians a temporary escape from their emotional straightjackets. It could be argued that the healthy release of inhibitions offsets any harm done to the liver.

Beer is the national drink. Like everything 100% Estonian, most breweries are owned by the Swedes and Finns. In beer cellars there are beer songs, beer jokes such as the (true) one about the blind man arrested twice for drunken driving, and beer snacks such as fried rye (black) bread served with sour cream and fresh garlic (called 'vampire's kiss' in one famous beer cellar), salted broad beans cooked in bacon fat, and succulent, barley-studded blood (black) pudding.

Bread beer – *Kali* – is mildly alcoholic (1%-2%) and is made from a fermentation of black bread, yeast and water with added fruit such as raisins and juniper berries. Innocuous traditional juices are made from redcurrants or cranberries and much is still home brewed. Tree devotees drink birch juice, *kasemahl*. Wines made from indigenous fruit and veg – beet, parsnip, berries – are deceptively potent.

> **66** *Viin* (vodka) reigns supreme among spirits (the kind that come in a bottle). **99**

Viin (vodka) reigns supreme among spirits (the kind that come in a bottle) and, whereas the Italians and French have 'table' wine or wine 'boxes', the Estonians have 'table' vodka or vodka 'boxes'. There is a moonshine version of vodka (called *puskar*) but as it may be concocted from truly unholy mixtures of medicines, aftershave, illegally produced spirit or fire-lighting fuel, it will rot the guts of even the strongest SOKs.

At least three (thwarted) attempts have been made to build a bootleg vodka pipeline from Russia (where vodka is much cheaper) that have involved ingenuity and engineering prowess on both sides of the border. These experiments are living proof that there is hope yet for convivial Estonian-Russian relations based on mutual interests.

Systems

Travel and transport

Driving is best approached as a challenge. The main highway between the two major cities, Tallinn and Tartu, is called 'the road of death'. Minor roads, despite the best effort of the Estonians (aided by EU funding), are still fundamental affairs, and harsh winters result in even poorer road conditions. The upside is that you are unlikely to meet anyone on country roads for hours.

> **❝ Driving is best approached as a challenge. The main highway between the two major cities, is called 'the road of death'. ❞**

There is a stalwart camaraderie on the road: a car travelling in the opposite direction will flash its lights if the police are about. And, if your car slithers off an icy road, most Estonians will stop, ask if you need help, and even attempt to drag your vehicle out of the ditch with ancient ropes kept in the boot in case there isn't a tractor handy.

When planning a journey it's important to remember to schedule your trip between festivals when bandstands and choir stages straddle the main roads and traffic lights are switched off. Whatever your reason for travel, the Estonians cannot conceive that it could possibly be more important than music and song.

Buses, trolleybuses, trams and trains run on time, even in blizzards and in the middle of nowhere.

Estonians know exactly when public transport vehicles are due to arrive and get to the stop approximately 30 seconds beforehand.

The old Soviet electric trains are still in operation. The train interiors have been re-vamped and there are three classes: the first class carriage has comfy seats, Internet access, newspapers, coffee served by waiters, and is stuffed with Estonian businessmen; the second class carriages have comfy seats and are stuffed with academics reading books; the third class carriages sport the original bum-numbing seats with half an inch of sponge covered in brown plastic and are stuffed with impecunious pensioners and students.

> **66 The Estonians' attitude to work is bi-polar. 99**

Public transport is efficient and inexpensive. If you're off to visit Jaan in his solitary farmhouse 40 kilometres from Hapsalu, you'll be able to get to the nearest village without too much trouble. You may need to walk the last few kilometres but, if you are lucky, you'll get a lift in a truck from an obliging local who may be delivering pigs. Just expect more communication from the pigs than from the driver.

Manual labour and manufacturing

The Estonians' attitude to work is bi-polar. On the one hand, they value honest hard work like logging or building roads. They are seldom lazy and can be very task-orientated and focused, especially in the short summer when the rush is on to get outdoor work done. Estonians will work a manic 14-hour day to finish a job quickly. If building a new highway means a 50-kilometre detour for road users, then the common good overrides any nuisance caused to individuals.

On the other hand, lurking inside every Estonian seems to be a lord or lady of the manor trying to get out. When, for instance, the detested statues of Lenin were taken down all over the Baltic States, the Lithuanians tore them down with their bare hands. The Latvians measured the offending objects, sought out a suitably sized lorry and crane and removed them themselves. The stately Estonians hired a private firm to do the deed, preferring the unpleasantness to be handled by a third party.

66 Lurking inside every Estonian seems to be a lord or lady of the manor trying to get out. 99

Small and medium enterprises (SMEs) make up 76% of the manufacturing sector. These beaver away all over Estonia in sectors such as light engineering (with a high degree of IT bits), farming, handicrafts and logging for the Finnish paper industry.

Many Estonian-owned enterprises are run by kin. Keeping business in the family satisfies the respect for "we do it like this". It also addresses Estonian anxieties about outsiders since, in theory, cousin Margit (twice removed) is less likely to run off with the takings.

Foreign investors are a family of sorts – kith rather than kin – because they usually come from nearby Scandinavia. A good example of a successful foreign-owned SME employing Estonians is Wendre which makes pillows and blankets. It's one of the suppliers to Ikea.

66 Estonians understand hierarchies – they were at the bottom of several for centuries. 99

Estonians understand hierarchies – they were at the bottom of several for centuries. A typical Estonian-owned company has a director, a manager and a few workers, all related to one another by blood or marriage and arranged in descending pecking order. All live in fear of the firm's equivalent of pensioner-elder Auntie Alma.

Business conduct is brisk and to the point. If you have arranged to meet someone, they will show up on time smartly dressed. If the meeting was scheduled for 11.00 and no-one arrives by 11.10 and you haven't had a call to your mobile to say that the individual has been abducted by pirates in the Gulf of Arabia while on a business trip, then your contact is dead. There is no other reason an Estonian would miss the opportunity to make money.

Some Estonians dream of earning a Porsche profit from the sale of a box of matches. Their role model is a character in Estonian folklore called Ants (Hans) nicknamed '*kaval*' (crafty) – the epitome of 'native cunning'. Kaval Ants starts out poor and ends up rich with no other help than the sharpness of his wits.

Should their own ingenuity fall short of the mark, the would-be millionaires can fall back on a multitude of youthful experts, products of the boom in business courses, whose laptops come as part of the uniform. Some would argue that there are fast becoming more experts than business people.

Links to the east

The nation's geographical location and relationship to the sea are both a blessing and a curse. The deep-sea waters of the capital's port are ice free and thus open for trade all year round, making Tallinn a jewel in the Baltic crown. It is also what attracted invaders and made the Russians eager to keep control of Estonia. China is the latest interested partner in the potential of Estonia's seaboard. The quantity

> **❝ The nation's geographical location and relationship to the sea are both a blessing and a curse. ❞**

of goods now transported by sea from the Far East to Moscow via Estonia is rising every year, in particular oil products, fertilizer, chippings and coal.

The harbours also deal with ro-ro (roll-on/roll-off) goods. This does not refer to inebriated Finns but to industrial, agricultural and recreational vehicles, although ro-ro ferries also carry foot passengers (including inebriated Finns).

Links to the land

Most Estonians still believe that earning your daily bread by cultivating the earth or harvesting the sea is the natural order of things. Their name for themselves before they became 'Estonians' (after the Aestii mentioned in a Roman history) was *maa rahvus*, 'the people of the land'.

> **Calling someone a peasant would never be a put-down in Estonia.**

Calling someone a peasant would never be a put-down in Estonia. Not that life on the land was ever easy – the cultivation period is very short, there is much un-drained bog and the soil is poor and littered with rocks that need removing before a plough can do anything useful. There are so many boulders and stones that Estonians still say "*Kivi kotti!* Stone in the bag!" when they want to wish someone good luck. Nonetheless, there is still a strong affection for the time when most Estonians were farmers even if life was lived at subsistence level. These days, however, if truth is told, playing Sudoku on the puzzle pages of *Maaleht*, the country life newspaper, is about as near to the soil as many Estonians are going to get.

Education

Estonians have computerised their education system. Estonian parents can have their children's grades, absences and even homework timetables sent to their mobile phones. Connecting to instruction over the ether without resorting to a live, salary-requiring classroom teacher satisfies two major Estonian objectives – success through learning without excessive pressure on the purse strings. Parents can relax knowing that when the temperature is -20° there is no necessity to take the tractor out of the garage to get little Juku to school over the frozen landscape. Juku himself can learn about the birds and bees from the comfort of his desk rather than behind a prickly juniper bush beside grandma's malodorous rural outhouse. Computer classes are the favourite lessons, and Estonia could well become the first nation to replace schoolbooks with microchips.

> **"Estonia could well become the first nation to replace schoolbooks with microchips."**

Such is the thirst for academic knowledge for some that they attain 'eternal student' status and are still doing physics equations in their heads whilst wrapping their own progeny against the cold and dropping them off at the nursery on their way to lectures.

Non-academic skills are developed in 'hobby' institutions financed jointly by government, voluntary organisations and parents. Sport and music are the most popular and almost every child belongs to a school choir, a band or an orchestra. Many Estonians remain keen members of some sort of amateur musical group all their lives.

An IT Government

The Estonian government is a standard model of western democracy. Every four years citizens participate in elections for the 101-member parliament (*riigikogu*) which then elects a president, a Head of State who has influence and authority rather than actual power. The Presidential office is much respected – a hangover from the days when the post holder was known as 'the state elder' – even if individuals cannot abide the incumbent.

> **❝ Estonia does not need a battery of bureaucratic bums on seats because it's a world leader in virtual democracy. ❞**

The Estonian civil service, local and central, is a lean machine – a mere 1.8% of the population. Estonia does not need a battery of bureaucratic bums on seats because it's a world leader in virtual democracy. Cyber-savvy citizens love their smart ID cards and one of the things they can do with them is vote.

The Estonian love affair with the ease and accessibility of information technology goes right to the top. The Prime Minister holds Cabinet meetings without printed documents. Those members out of town can log on and join in. After a decision is made it's disseminated to the populace via the net within 30 seconds. This saves time, effort and, most importantly, trees. The only downside is that to bring the country to a standstill, all you would need to do is organise a power cut.

Foes today, friends tomorrow

The political scene veers towards a 'two Estonians, five opinions' scenario. Once nearly 30 parties – the blues, the greens, the reds, the bright yellow with pink spots – contested seats. Power brokers have now boiled them down to six main ones.

Since the electoral system is proportional, no single party ever has enough seats to govern alone and all administrations have formed coalitions in a political version of musical chairs. Opponents during a campaign can become eternal allies the day after the votes are counted (until the next election). This is not disastrous as all parties are rather alike (being largely liberal-minded, paternalistic free marketeers), so there is a high degree of consensus on fundamental issues.

> **66 Parliamentary debates are like watching paint dry. 99**

Parliamentary debates are like watching paint dry. Ministers are expected to be jowly, stony faced and have tons of gravitas. Lively opposition is not the Estonian way. This is not just another manifestation of the Estonian distaste for conflict. Most political players are ex-Communist Party members, a history that does not stimulate scintillating oratory. Expediency dictates that there will be no return to full-blown communism. An academic spoke for the nation when he declared "Defending the old communist system is the only service an Estonian will not sell you for any price."

Crime & Punishment

The law

The Estonian legal system is largely derived from a German tradition. The Estonian attitude, however, is radically different from that of the obedient, law-abiding Germans. There are very few petty regulations and those there are (usually compulsory EU imports, and anything with a 'Union' tag is automatically suspect) are quite often simply ignored. This is because Estonians are unused to a nanny state – the USSR didn't care much what happened if Margus fell off a scaffold or there was no warning signal to tell Juku or Merii-liin when a train was due on the track.

> **66 There are very few petty regulations and those there are are quite often simply ignored. 99**

Cops and robbers

The Estonian police are a modern, well-equipped, multi-ethnic organisation of a standard comparable to most western European law enforcement agencies. Unlike many ex-Soviet countries, it is rare to hear of cases of corruption. The rapid formation of a police choir and brass band helped to assure Estonians that, although the rookies were callow and inexperienced, they were loyal to the new nation.

Respect for the police may be growing, but the Estonians have never quite shaken off centuries as frontier country – for the Holy Roman, the Swedish and the Soviet Empires – and they have a lingering soft spot for the freewheeling, self-reliant outlaw. In 2000 the nation cheered the Voitka brothers, petty criminals described by their admirers as 'freedom fighters', 'forest brothers' and 'pro-anarchists' who had successfully evaded capture for 14 years by the best efforts of both Soviet and Republican forces. "It's just like a song festival," crowed one newspaper headline as the boys in blue finally began to close in on the errant pair. "Only mulled wine was missing."

Tree-son

Some of the most serious public censure has been for crimes against trees. The police caught a 74-year-old in the act of felling a defenceless birch in a cemetery. Whilst crimes such as theft are reluctantly accepted as normal, the Estonians were clearly horrified by this atrocity and did not hesitate to have the miscreant referred instantly to a psychiatrist.

Punishment

The Estonian prison population is less than 1% of the population. There are five prisons dotted around the country and they're not holiday camps. Many Estonians cannot see a need for concern about poor conditions or lack of any meaningful social work support for those found guilty of anti-social behaviour. They lean towards pagan values when it comes to criminal justice. Only the restraining hand of EU legislature prevents the local lads from apprehending wrong doers and roasting them (without trial) alive on a spit, just like the ancestors did.

Language & Ideas

While many languages are concise, Estonian represents a higher order of brevity. The result is a level of linguistic sophistication that makes it one of the world's more difficult tongues to master. Estonians consider their language to be a form of 'protection' and the main reason that the nation retained its identity during foreign occupation. Outsiders might suggest that its degree of difficulty was what did the trick.

> **While many languages are concise, Estonian represents a higher order of brevity.**

There are a number of phrases typical of the language, each of which is illustrative of the way the speakers think as well as the way they talk. So, for drinking, Estonians can choose just the right word not only to describe the effects of intoxication, but also where on the scale of intoxication a person is. For example, to say '*temal on aurud peas*' means 'he's got steam in his head' – a reference to moderate drunkenness. However if the phrase is '*tema on täis*' it means he is filled with booze from head to toe. Being '*tais*' (full) is different to having *aurud peas* (steam in your head) because *tais* people tend to sit in the corner looking unsteady and half asleep, while those with *aurud peas* are still touched with a boisterous air and party mood that has yet to progress to a headache-inducing stupor once the steam of happiness has evaporated.

Then there is '*peapesu*' or 'head laundry'. If you give someone a *peapesu* it means you've given them a piece of your mind,

> **66 The word evokes the idea of shoving a person's head in a bowl and washing all the stupidity out of it. 99**

usually in a fairly forceful fashion. To an Estonian, the word evokes the idea of shoving a person's head in a bowl and washing all the stupidity out of it.

Although there is now a standard Estonian language, it was cobbled together out of two basic dialects (north and south) by increasingly desperate foreigners trying to communicate. Estonian grammar is, consequently, a nightmare. The noun has fourteen declensions. Adjectives are no better. The grammar book can chirp cheerfully that 'only in four cases does the adjective fail to take the same case as the noun' but remembering what four cases take a maverick genitive, let alone why, is just one of the joys of learning a language that is basically arcane and has never been fully codified.

The verb has no future tense *per se* and there is no subjunctive mode (that expresses hope or possibility). The conditional tense is used for something that could take place and the oblique mode is used to indicate actions that supposedly occur but of which the speaker has no direct knowledge – thus *Ta olevat halb inimene*, 'I have heard he is a rotter but as I have no direct knowledge of this person I cannot say for sure.' This hesitancy to commit oneself is common, and a natural distrust of positivism was not helped by the compulsory optimism of the Soviet system. Estonians never hurry to affirm or negate anything. Instead of 'yes' or 'no' they prefer to say: *küllap vist* ('probably, I dare say') and, of course, *ootame, vaatame*.

> **❝ Estonians never hurry to affirm or negate anything. Instead of 'yes' or 'no' they prefer to say: 'probably, I dare say'. ❞**

The sound of Estonian is beautiful – 'the language of the birds' as poets have called it – but spoken Estonian is tortuous. The alphabet has 32 characters with nine vowels, 36 diphthongs and even a few triphthongs. Whole phrases in Estonian can exist without consonants: *aoäia õe uue oaõieaia õueaua ööau* translates as 'the night-honour of a watching dog in the garden of fresh bean-flowers belonging to the sister of my sunrisy father-in-law' should you ever need to impart such knowledge. Both consonants and vowel sounds come in three lengths: short, long, and extra-long. Getting pronunciation right requires years of fancy mouth work and no dental braces.

The mother tongue

Estonian poetry is full of the love of beauty – *ilo*. *Ilo* is what makes life worthwhile: it is the feeling at the song festivals great and small and signifies what Estonians still know – that, despite the necessity for money, the best things in life are free.

Ilo is the solitary candle in the window in winter darkness, the tea light in the old oak in the middle of nowhere in spring, the little bunch of flowers on the tablecloth, the ears of wheat on a weather-beaten

> **❝ *Ilo* is the solitary candle in the window in winter darkness, the tea light in the old oak in the middle of nowhere in spring... ❞**

old stone, a tintinnabuli Pärt cadence. These exquisite miniatures are the Estonians' natural responses to timeless, ancient beauty, responses that have survived, unchanged, centuries of slavery and oppression. It is for *ilo* that one's admiration for the Estonians creeps up on little cat feet wrapped up in the mist from the Baltic Sea.

Ilo is the echo of distant Arcadia, of a world young and unspoilt that the Estonians have cherished, come hell or high water, for more than 10,000 years. They do it like that, you see.

The Authors

Of Estonian and Lithuanian parentage, **Hilary Bird** grew up in Britain. After a long career in public service, a search for her roots led her to Estonia. She now lives in Tartu and commutes to London, leaving her Estonian cat in the care of angel neighbours. For silence and solitude she escapes to her *suvila* by the Baltic with her laptop and gallons of insect repellent. There she addresses the head-banging complexities of the mother tongue, then changes to soothing English to pen her regular column for ex-pat Estonians, *Bird Droppings*.

Ulvi Mustmaa (which means Blackland) grew up in Soviet Estonia but likes the current one better. Her work in the travel industry gives her opportunities undreamed of in her youth when a working trip to a communal farm in the Caucasus was as good as it got. In addition to some Christmas song lyrics, she is the author of a veritable mine of hilarious information about the habits of Latvians called, with typical Estonian directness, *Latvian Stories*.

Lembit Öpik, the son of Estonian parents whose family left Estonia to escape Stalin, was born in Northern Ireland and is a Member of Parliament for Montgomeryshire, Wales. Apart from a glamorous social life, he is also known for his TV appearances on programmes such as *Question Time* and *Have I Got News For You.*

He has a pilot's licence and is a keen astronomer with a special interest in asteroids that could collide with the Earth. His grandfather, Ernst Öpik, was a notable astronomer and astrophysicist after whom the Öpik-Oort Cloud is named, as is asteroid 2099 Öpik.

In 1998, while para-gliding in the remote Welsh mountains, he had his own collision with Earth. He broke his back in twelve places, as well as his ribs, sternum and jaw, shattered his knees and lost six teeth. Faced with death, he had no choice but to walk to safety. It was an ordeal worthy of the Son of Kalev (see page 11), but one that he says was less traumatic than writing about the Estonians.

Xenophobe's®
guides

Xenophobe's®
lingo learners

 Speak the lingo by speaking English. "

O
Oval Books

5 St John's Buildings Canterbury Crescent London SW9 7QH